AF335062

Gallery Books
Editor: Peter Fallon

A RAFT FROM FLOTSAM

John Jordan

A Raft from Flotsam

Versifications 1948-1974

Gallery Books

A Raft from Flotsam is published with the assistance of An Chomhairle Ealaíon (The Arts Council of Ireland) in a limited edition of 1,000 copies, 225 of which are bound in cloth and signed by the author, by

The Gallery Press,
19, Oakdown Road,
Dublin 14, Ireland.

Cover artwork by Michael Kane

Acknowledgements

Acknowledgements are made to the editors of *Aquarius* (London), *Broadsheet, The Dublin Magazine, The Lace Curtain* and *New Irish Writing* (The Irish Press) in which some of these poems have appeared.

Contents

In memory of Enid Starkie (1897-1970)
and Robert MacBryde (1913-1966)
both of whom asked me to sing
a song, do a dance or
write a book

Pub Poem of the '40s

i.
"Come, come, come!"
   Cry the Men of God,
And why in God's name don't I go?
But other mummers die
And the doxies they cry,
There are more things in life,
Than brass tacks and a wife.

"Come, *do* come!"
   Cry the Painted Men,
But why in God's name don't I go?
For me that mummer died,
For me his mother cried :
There are worse sides to death
Than rouge and baited breath.

The solution might be
To make a pass
At a decent, healthy,
Catholic lass,
With desirable paps
And intriguing thighs
And imbecility in her eyes.

To settle down (but where?)
Outside the town's the thing
And you'll always sing
If you're early to bed
And late to rise — and
What a simply smashing surprize,
When on a cold dark winter's night
She coyly whispers that the prize
Of strictly modest copulation
Is a Blessed Event — ah what elation!
For we shall have done our duty!
And as everyone knows
(Including that priest with the mottled nose,
That charming thing who gave me a rose,
The boy who at Seapoint was chary
The Scouts and Gampdom of Sairey)
Duty is beauty!

ii.
But rarely, perhaps, to go alone,
Alone on days with mist
When the glass moon comes early
And unseen gulls skim phantom
Barks that bear across the darkish water
My dear unreasonable courtesans.
Their milk is gamey
Smacking of fried fish and future pain.
They travel far with easy hearts,
And forget with whom they've lain.

Into the train!
Home to the daughter of J. J. Quinn
Home to the love that's free from sin,
And the Pope has sent us his blessing!
(Conveyed by the Bishop of Nara)

"Pray for the Pope's intentions"
"The Fires of Hell" said Father Molloy
While in the front row squinting at a boy,
Sat Kate who is a modest dove
Well-grounded in the perils that attend Free Love,
But not as nice as Peggy P.,
Who in one's green days use to be
A good-time girl with risky males
And quite a dab at dubious tales:
In fact she held the bed quite dear,
But finished up with a skipping queer.
"Three Hail Marys for the Conversion of Russia."

iii.
There was thin blue light
Where some stars had upstaged
The clouding glass moon.
It annexed partially from the night
A fairly classic head, blonde hair,
A nape ending in shadows.

The rain had spiked us
Bone had gone to marrow-fat,
Eye to eye had grown unlike,
There were new hard pebbles in love's pockets.

The wind had towelled us,
Back to bone went attainable flesh
Limb grew to limb again familiar.
Lovers whisper their assuring axioms
Forget that the weather can catch them out,
Bodies come together as perfect strangers,
Terrified, mysterious, until the death in doubt.

iv.
Wake my love no more in nightmare,
Devil-goats should not be near,
When inside my arms I hold you,
Unless it is myself you fear.
Fear perhaps may be contagious,
Even when creatures are at peace:
Sometimes, child, I fear to lose you,
Since flesh, being weak, must beg release.

v.
Flesh calls to flesh across the ramparts
Built by some spirit to protect its love,
But an aureate head may spin a halo
Persuading flesh that spirit has removed,
Tenanted another fleshy habitation
Where for a new death we're on probation.
Since each loss erases past possession,
We find that love has missed the bus,
And solitary, since we left the womb,
Romance up the night as personal doom.
There is some hope for little Peggy P.
But God of Love, is there any hope for me?

vi.
The Painted Men grow old,
Cold invades the veins
Where the blood of strangers pulses.
Clay triumphs over alchemy,
Brimstone guts the dressing-table.

But their plumes still wave
Above the screaming trees,
Wave their signal of unending love.
The glass moon, their complacent madame
Smiles, so tender, on their follies,
The stars shine for them
A macula especially.

But don't forget to pray for the Pope's Intentions,
Every single Sunday the P.P. mentions
Nuns, priests, abroad are very badly pressed
Bringing God to black babies and ensuring they're
        dressed.
Yes. Pray too for the destruction of the Reds,
For all poor occupants of unchaste beds,
For disgraceful dipsos, sods, and tarts,
Joyces, Gides, and Jean-Paul Sartres.

And may Christ have mercy on us all.

Dublin 1948

Notes for an Obscene Sequence

The silver fox, my darling,
Will gobble up your breast,
O strip yourself, come quick with me,
Be naked, that's the test.

Our trees of iron are just as fine
As shoots of flowering shrubs,
The martinis of my kisses
As good as gin in pubs.

You'll soon forget the pleasure-trips
To Mayo or Shanghai,
But in the end you'll always feel
My hand upon your thigh.

So throw away the chicken-legs,
Come fasten on my mouth,
And when you're glutted there, my bird,
We'll take a trip down South.

Dublin 1948

First Letter: To Donal O'Farrell

Do you remember?
We share one basket and I dip to find
Me a schoolboy, primfaced, soft, refined,
Some said sexless, some said unkind,
Mouth twisted by a hymn to gods I didn't know about.
Did you? odd goblin friend, wan as a straw
Craning your neck like a swan in the straw,
— Reeds in the canal in the sun are like straw —
Opening your mouth to say "maw" instead of "more"
— Did you?

Do you remember the sun atoming the dust
Of green, of blue maps, of salmon-pink squares,
The white mixed grill of Hall and Knight,
Chill, chaste Euclid, that swan who ticked off Ptolemy?
Do you remember our great blind mother
And her servant crows who beaded eyes
On us canaries in her leaky chalk-fumed cage?
Our first silk-light knowledge of *lacrimae*,
Virgil born by the long green fat canal?
Your elucidation of my heart's eccentric page?

Of course we'd have been better
Playing manly games,
"Knicks, knicks, football-boots and jerseys,"
To have known the frenzy of boot and ball
Like all the forgotten lads who
Yelped above at their pigeon in the placid grey,
The unknown lads whose old men's memories
Will kindle the damp sod,
Mud-caked knickers and dungy boots,
Their brothers' hortations at the end of day.
And I think of you now and
Find me a schoolboy — have you forgotten,
And will you still forget,
Like the swan in the straw
(Reeds in the canal in the sun are like straw)
But no more.

Dublin 1948

Second Letter: To Patrick Swift

Dear P.,
      This letter may explain better
      than words of the mouth,
      words, words, words,
      that soothed our drought
      through rain and stars,
      the mockery of dawn,
      we cold as the trees.

For you must keep in mind
that we are less than kin,
but more than kind, for

      While you were ranting your lyceum lines
      careering the vaults of your glittering dooms,
      bleeding at the heart from paper knives
      I have my nuances and Chekovian glooms—
      But we were both mummers, and so we got on.

      Mine was a mime of lime-scent and heart-break
      quiet, frail, imbecile, thirsty for applause
      — and O you knew that and nurtured me, because —
      Thespis's children stick together
      in sunlight and shower and weather
      when the proud rose must surely fall,
      thrown on a dump with all the rest of the trappings,

            the split gold tights
            the ragged brocade gown
            the mothy ermine choker
            the sweet tinsel crown

      and our cascades of pasten jewels,
      bright as tears,
      worthless as tears,
      your tears,
      my tears.

      Yes, mine was a mime of lime-scent and quiet heart
      yours one of cypresses, and blood on the snow
      but we both were mummers and didn't care to know,

to realize,
to dig,
 to pick away the paint,
to clutch the hand lovingly
around the white skull.
Skull last seen in the dead of night
or glimpsed at waking in the submarine light,
skull precious ivory,
to be kissed and touched tenderly . . .

As you may have noticed
the games are done
and I for one, my friend, am very tired.
I must confess, too, I find it hard
not to have regrets,
for years spent in plays
so unworthy of our talents.

It will be difficult to adapt ourselves to
ordinary life. And of couse we'll always be
peculiar, rearing the head, pouting the
lips, stancing the body, when a stranger
comes into the room. You know that as well
as I do.
                Yours,
                John Jordan.

Dublin 1948

An Old Letter

To begin with and in a manner of speaking
We live in the trenches.
You are on leave in the sunlight.
Your wine glitters because it seems unending
And is unending, the heart at peace being cretinous,
Careless as child in cinema darkness.
                        I say "Careless"
But knowing you, knowing
The craters that lie before you even beneath
Crisp waters when you drift amber,
Darkness that snuffs scarlet green and golden rockets
I should say "careful".
And I see you with care, with tenderness,
Swallowing the ruby on diapered terraces
Slowly and grave entering the sheets,
Your careful rapture as you explore again love's valleys,
The mysterious woods where peace should be.

But yet you are on leave in the temporary sunlight,
I cannot expect you, but do with all my heart,
To figure the oil and the dirt, the pus-smells,
Our bloody dreams, not of the temporary sunlight
Nor the deathless ruby, nor love's valleys
Nor mysterious woods where peace should be,
But wood-glow and tea-cups, door against the rain,
The wind noises, the dependable window-panes.
I want you to know how we wake
To the stench of tears, bloody sweat,
Eyes, heels, sore from the narrow patrols,
Lips smarted from incautionary kisses.

Perhaps that's taking it to the fair,
For we are not really in the trenches.
How you'll smile when I tell you:
No oil, no blood, no uncommon dirt here
But gradated greenery
And tranquil at the top of the garden
A green cushion, an orange chair,
A woman, a man, a boy, like you in the sunlight
But screened by pied lilac.
To end with and in a manner of speaking
I love you and we live in the trenches.

19

London 1951

Wordsworth Was Right

"At eight-thirty a.m.
A Titian-headed girl
Said good-bye to her mother
Going down the steps
Through yellow light and the trees
Away to the beaches and May."

"That's beautiful". And the way she says it,
Her eyes all warmth, you'd think
She surely meant it.
What's the purpose of the lie.
What's the purpose of the great room,
Where the trailing cobweb glistens
And the ghosts tap their bones on the piano-lid,
Shuffle the sheets of Debussy, and the dust
Settling . . . . . .
Do you know what I mean?

What too's the purpose of training American glory
Under subtle pretence of business and the like . . .
Yet was that glory sweeter than the violets
Wet, wet violets sold in Stephen's Green,
Gentler, sharper, sharper than the candle-flame,
Candle guttering in Pembroke Road.

Listen people . . . . .
Only he could tell us the truth about it all:
The man who worried epic out of the sod
Stamped on the ashes till they glowed
The man who gleaned the lyric at the heart of the clod
The man who reaped what he sowed.
But how well we know, yes, what he would say,
Crashing through the cobwebs (lovely cobwebs!) to the
    fine raw day.
Listen people . . . . .
"That's not poetry! Pure shite,
             pure shite!"

"Yes Patrick. That's very well put. But
Don't you think . . . . ."
"The Muse is queer. She's like a goad.
Poetry's never written unless a man's
All on fire to do it, on fire with
Happi-
         ness, on fire with
Sor-
     row."

O to get out of it
O to get out of it
O to get out of it
Or drink the Shannon dry!

Ah the eyes are warm again and the May days
Have come back to the room.
Crackling paper, spilling water,
Beautiful shades out of business.
Ah the eyes are warm again,
"Read us another one John".

"At four-thirty a.m.
A white-haired woman
Said good-bye to guests
Leading them down the steps
Through the night-stock fragrance
Out into the reaches of November".

Dublin 1948

A Seduction of the '40s

She was a fine girl, amber, supple,
He was a real fine boy, long-lashed.
She said to him one night
      (When they were ending a chat
        About Pico—him with the Golden Hair)
She said to him one night:
"Come up, come see me one night"
The trouble was they both had brains.
So he went up to see her one night.
She had a very nice flat
With lamp-shades designed special
And a photo signed *le gach deá-ghuí*
By an Irish actor and rows and rows of books.

There was a balcony too and they looked down into the
        garden
And he said, "You know, darling,
Your breasts, I mean bosom, is like apples."
She said "Don't give me that crap."
They'd both seen Bogey in *Casablanca.*

She was a great girl and they had six gins with orange.
She said, "I do think you've got a tiny waist for a man."
So it went on to 2 a.m.
He stood up, took off his jacket,
Went to the window and said,
      "Let us walk out where people look out
        On trees and flowers and wonderful affairs,
        And never look in on death and sin,
        Excrement of the unspeakable mind,
        Insolent bully"
Or words to that effect.
And she said "Gee."
He sat down beside her, put his hand on her bosom.
It opened out to him
Not at all like pippins.
She said, "You'll have to leave."
So it went on to 3 a.m.
He stood up, took off his shirt.
Dixit: Now that the sleeping time is come
And love's musk scents the air

Let us lie down and cease to wear
Our bottoms out in foolish talk,
Masochistic jabbing.
Dixit: I don't like the use of that word 'bottom'.
Dixit: It's about time we
Learnt that the heart's no pincushion.

And then, you know, he put out the light,
And they went to bed and were unhappy everafter.

Dublin 1948-49

Trahison des Clercs

for Pearse Hutchinson

Some people that you know,
An old woman peeved by defeat,
A sex-meshed codger,
Whose heart does not go,
A subtle sunshine boy, one sleepy eye on "every
     main chance,"
Have abused you, all three in a row.
And I because of a secret low allegiance
To a six-hour day, a cushioned chair,
Enough cash to be able to save,
Have been silent.

Dublin 1949

A Dialogue

for Justin Keating

A: If wicked men came
      Down the aisle through oaken benches,
      Eager to rip the golden vestments,
      To desecrate the Body,
      Crumble the wafers with wax and petals,
      What would you do?
      Would you stand up for the Son of God?
      Would you let that boy's blood out
      On the clattering marble,
      Be beaten with gun-butts or convenient rods?
      Would you cheer up the Liberators?

B: Perhaps you'd be happy with your darling
      In the great white cities,
      Clean and smooth, poplar-lined.
      In the nights of ordered passion
      You'd beget children for whom lice
      Are creatures like the dinosaur.

      Could you face it?

C: I will too. Hack this mind
      Into biddability.
      Hear no more the whinge
      Of faith's Samsonite children.
      Walk steadily ahead, eyeless for
      The blue grotto and green pasture
      Projected by the Credos.
      I will go.

Dublin 1949

The Chime

for B. G. Achong

Talking is as bad as not talking.
Silence is as perilous as speech.
Between the chinks of speech
Falls the hail of silence.

Telling is as bad as not telling.
Confession posits standards,
Fouls up the wells of grief,
Each glance turns hazardous.

Vision is as bad as fancy.
Certain waiting as hard on the heart
As a squinting vigil with a clock.

Say then there's no difference
Between good-will and good-bye.
Quote deep sea and devil.
Say then there's no difference.
But the difference is music,
A class of chime,
Heard at all times, at all places.

Dublin 1951

An Imaginary Biography

i

He loved much in his youth,
Drank deeply from the wine
Vendible tepid summer evenings,
Those Georgian days in Kildare Street.

But at fifty,
His sisters nibbled their veils,
Splashed in their sherry,
Let crumbs of Marie biscuits
Drop, cling, in the red flannel
They wore for their chests.
Frail, merry, unaware of hell,
They were full of requests
That he'd take a wife, so
Keep the stock alive, for
They had married one and all,
Grown grey mice, and small,
Known only the rind of motherhood:
Julia, Sally and Rose
Bought cousins' babies clothes,
And dandled changelings
At their player breasts.
On the whole they were distraite
And after thirty years
Had grown somewhat tired
Of waiting their helpmates
Eat, sleep, shave,
Hearing them guffaw,
Drunkenly weep, of
Lying by blocks of lard,
Cold, dry, hard,
Cold as their seed.

ii

Year by year they went,
Julia, Sally and Rose,
With crocuses and happy rain,
A minimum of mourning,
An excess of whiskey, and
   Their husbands said they'd loved them.

But still he was single:
Happy but for a thin pain
That caught him in the small
Of his back — that was all.

He took to gin and frolics,
He read enormous tomes,
For he was a scholarly man,
Knew Greek, dreamed of Japan.
They all said, "He is failing."
How could he have health
Scooping tinned salmon in a stuffy room?
He would wear his heart out on drink,
Die on the road without a priest
To speed him to the brink
Of plum-blossom land where *Iosagán* is so pretty.

They were wrong.
Dying he heard the hot song
Of thrushes from the Sisters' garden.
In a warm lavender room
With window blinds called fawn,
A flowery chamber-pot and every dawn,
The loony chime of a landing-clock,
He dreamed the journey of his days
Glancing out at all the ways
He'd met with beauty:
Shriven, he saw beneath the skin
Of those he'd loved and lusted,
Could not quite consider sin
Moments when he'd trusted,
Staked his immortal soul
On an eyelash flicker,
Rose to glory on the pediment of despair.

One dawn that spring, plum-blossom invaded his
     room,
The crazy clock shrilled through the percolated
     gloom,
And then onwards his peace was quite extra-
     ordinary.

Dublin 1950

Homage to the Pseudo-Jansenius

The faithful, quite rightly, will not listen to reason.
From the hubris of innocence they know
The path to be as narrow as the gate.
They forsake all forms of richness
Since wavering for creatures
Most certainly entails being late,
Breaking and entering the preserves of the elect,
The pinched, fearful of fantasy,
Disdainful of cakes and ale,
The true passengers.

All the rest of it is maculate:
Clerical quip and liberal mind,
Perspectives of eternity which we're told
Art can find—
Christian Plato, the stretching by fly boys of Thomas the Ox.

The rub lies with the distant honeys,
Sienese cheek-bones, Buonarotti hips,
Challenge the Rock of Ages,
Damned by tenderness, we turn asterisked pages,
Will never, though, live, adore, be luminous
Out of this world and time.

Dublin 1950

Non Dicam

The decision has been made: I shall not tell you.
Fear, toilet-trained now, has spliced my tongue.
Fear of same debâcle as other loves' recitals,
Nasty and brutish the Leviathan of disdain.

As things are at least the knowledge,
The presence of a friable decision,
Feathery images of sesamatic words
Make tolerable a yen for sweet permission.

But dear thing must I attend
A quarantine of a lustrum
Because the hound pounces on to its desire?
Can nothing in my bearing
Key you to the cypher,
Pull out the bloody plug before there's fire?

But the decision has been taken
Resolve must not be shaken
By casual affection in your tones.
I must feed in isolation
Prune ramblers of elation
Snip all Aves and Vales
And breast-buds when I see you all alone.

Vingt ans après
In clockish time some sixty hours,
Tongue has jerked the splice,
Has opened pain.
The decision has been broken
Though to you I have not spoken.
The mines are flooded, Christ,
It's dark again.
I must build a raft from flotsam,
The vomit in the belly
Time may clear away,
Mens insana too, will perhaps be sane.
I sight already wrack, suitably inadequate,
I'll work it out in shanties,
And brave again skin-diving in the main.

Vingt ans après
In clockish time some sixty hours,
I have found coral, amber, excrement,
Armour for another soft or squally day.
For which I am truly thankful,
And can hail you, o my dear,
Salve.

Dublin 1950

Gerard Dead 1

They told him at school about Voltaire,
How the Jesuits made much of him,
And the bright boy
Died a most horrible death.

Missioners from the pulpit warned him of pride,
Which might imperil his deathless soul,
Worse, worse than Tophet, the joy
Of choiring God be withheld.

Brothers, missionaries, a Russian salad of clerics,
Drove home His Bones and His Bloody Side,
His child-days were enlightened by baroque images
Of how gruesomely his Saviour Christ had died.

The 'orrible and disgusting details of His Death
Did not mark him nor the pathos of His Birth.
The game was worth no candles,
Candles to his gentle mother,
Heaven if anywhere lay, in bread and wine of earth.
But some candle near the heart was real,
Lit Gethsemene, lit Calvary,
Led him to kneel.

Dublin 1950

Song

Gone are my goblin and his fairy queen
To the shimmering city where I should have been
Had a hobgoblin not fed upon my heart
Gobbled all up a very big part,
Left me to cry on an English green,
In the shimmering city where I should have been.

London   July 9   1951

Gerard Dead 11

i.
Words, lint on wound, unwritten dedications,
Surrogate feeling, cramp in the night.
Still the true misery exists, burgeons,
The glittering ache of more fortunate
Lovers, mothers, authentic brothers:
Words dislocate local necessary pain.

ii.
Take those tulips festering in the death-room,
Crucial blossoms they celebrate the episode well-played,
This wood where we mourn the face we have made:
This is no dead boy but a Trojan shade,
At very least an infant from castellated Spain.

iii.
Words will not redeem our poor marionette,
The toy horse, wicker shoes, mauve light
Where Dietrich inspects, all plumes and ermine,
The mended linen where they have you lain.

vi.
The facts could not be a plain dead boy,
Who crooned in gutters with marbles in his fist,
Who perchance with innocence worked out a tryst,
Kept it through dog-days of beckoning hell,
Hurled Satchmo back at the passing bell.

v.
But o brother mine your false
Brother begs that you
Intercede, plead, give the info'
On what happened.
Beg salt for my eyes,
Gripe for my bowels.

London-Oxford   June 1951-November 1953

Fourth Letter: To David Posner

Dear D.,
        Because with you
Big Daddy, Justice, booms again,
Because with you the harvest of flails
Seeded by we little ones that confuse Cross and Tree,
Is again believable: I write to you.

You have known, I believe, the queasiness of Mass-time,
The temptation of solitude in the afternoon,
Nostalgia for unexplored elm-dark gardens,
That comes in with the First of Sacred June.
'The starveling is fed on Sunday mornings,
The sacred mops up the leaky profane,'
Yet *grand siécle* maxims, airs from Poulenc,
Shoot across the fresh interior rain.
You who would 'like to be forsaken
By tears that do not count'
Are right to have none of me
For whom the heart-strings are apron-strings,
Each romantic picnic a return
To summerdays, white lilac,
Sand-castles that, lackaday, seemed durable.

But don't bother your noddle,
I've long since mastered the role of Désolé,
(I've been quite a flop as Désiré),
I've learned from repertory the way to handle
Needless prompts from Will Hay.
Still because with you, that old bags, Mercy,
Sets up her stall in the High,
Cherubim and Seraphim
Are again believable: I write to you.
Believe me, that alone is why.

Oxford 1953

The Lance

Being of human kind
The spear in His Side
Brought nearer than in the strolling years
The uplifted foolish faces,
The jostling and wine-bibbing,
The touch of hot earth on His flesh,
The olive-oil and sweat smells of His people.
Perhaps with the purple flowed love
For the fig tree he blasphemed.

Oxford 1954

In the Nine Winters

In the nine winters of our discontent
We unflesh pity for a thorned motive
In new departures from required perfection,
Groping for succour of unsteady images
From childhood, death-bed, private blackness.
With these we sow the creepers of our giving,
Master our crabbish scuttle from taking.
"So long, God, and my Galatea
I've just noticed my heart is breaking."

So on we travel to the next shipwreck
Followed by the Fisherman's inland bird.
The creature's voluntary skewers the elegy
Sung in a fathom's knowledge of sinking,
Drowned for a hank of yellow coarse hair,
Marinated for a daub of love.
Dead lovers rise from new shipwrecks
Often and most amiably are drowned:
For their nine winters they dream the knowledge
That cock and gull make the same sound.
But Galatea and my God,
I'm presently waking.
Have you lost your senses?
My heart is breaking.

Oxford 1954

'Entre Chat et Loup'*

for Quentin Stevenson

Cry no more with cat and wolf
Roam no more about the gulf
Where the gallant go to dive
And being dead come back alive.

Send away the hearthside cat
Starve the wolf that did not bite.
Dive deep down for what you lack
Being alone you may come back.

Leave the twilight while you may
Find the day beyond the day
All that light that sharpens form,
Beats the wild thing back to norm.

Death is where they cannot give:
You must ask for grace to love
Far away from cat or wolf,
Dive quite alone into the gulf.

Oxford 1954

*Entre *chien* et loup: In the dusk of evening

One who was not Invited to the Opening of the Joyce Tower Complains Bitterly

They came:
Jesuits, judges, Telefís jokers,
Visiting firemen, Cork pipe-smokers,
Monumental patrons, U.C.D. wives:
Time O you *beast* you, despite your worst forgives.

They goggled:
Columnists, socialites, jolly old pals,
Round the clock drinkers, Trinity gals,
Play okay-ers, the Minister, *haute couturières:*
Time, O you *pup* you, has made you one of theirs.

They guzzled:
Doctors, lawyers, departmental bosses,
B.B.C. balladmen, drawn by lucky horses,
Socialists, capitalists, Fianna and Fine:
Time, O you *fiend* you, has put you back in line.

They went:
Piling into taxis, limousines and growlers,
Titivating tipsily the afternoon's howlers:

'God it must have cost
Scott a lot of lolly.
Tell me now boys,
Does he leave the key with Dolly?'

But O you man you
It was different in 'twenty-two
When few but Cons were pro
And most of the rest were anti.

Blanchardstown 1962

Note 1.2 'Telefís Eireann' is the official title of the Irish Television Service.
1.14 'Fianna Fail' and 'Fine Gael' are the Republic's chief political parties.
1.20 Mr. Michael Scott was the donor of the Tower.
1.22 Mrs. Dolly Robinson was the first Curator of the Tower.
1.25 'Con' is the familiar appellation of both Dr. A. J. Levanthal and the late Dr. C.P. Curran.

Tidings from Breda

i.
Sweating in my underclothes in Breda,
False Greco face mosquito-swollen,
A couple of thoughts laid a
Hand on me: indecent assault
On soul.

ii.
One man said, kindly Machiavel:
'Others have done what you have done,
Squandered talents, gone in for fun,
Outgrown wild oats, made a success.
In so many words, 'Get out of the mess.'
Spoken very wisely, not very well.

iii.
Wisdom smokes from the unstaked.
Good direction is morsed from the blinkered.
But mind you, I'm inclined
To think that an earlier season
Might have found me more receptive
When *couilles* and caul were of sturdier kind.

iv.
Everyman has a singular future.
Mine is failure. I'd better admit it.
It may suit you, wise men and bright girls
To wish on me flecks of glory.
But I am I. Alone I know
The facts. Jordan's Book of Records
Would shake you. My locks are gory.

v.
Barren, barren, barren:
The cicadas sing.
I've done my best these days to forget:
Lent my razor to Joaquín
(O the fruiting fig trees outside my window)
Discussed aesthetics with María Antonia,
High above the City of the Virgin:
I brought lost loved ones gossip and whiskey,

She crescented with child,
He waxed proud, bronzed, mythical,
Drunk Free Cubas with *La Barba*,
Heard, told tales of Señora Nati,
Was dropped at Prici's by Toni and Mati,
('You are too tall?' said Mati,
'You must rest more,' said Nati)
At four o'clock the roosters wake me.

vi.
Some good may come of this:
High above the City of the Virgin
La Barba Catalanized
The least favoured cygnet of
The Swan of Coolgreany.
An omen: light flickers,
Failure of power. Unlike that Swan
I'm slow at the go. Yet
Though he cackle at my mewling
I will not shy from his crackling.
Swans, one's told, have songs.
Pavlova bit the dust.

vii.
I have been cruel for twenty years
(Or nearly), douched desires
Of undesired, homely, mad, thick,
Pot rejecting kettle:
That club-footed Yank I unhearted
That breastless girl who
On a go-cart
Pushed her brats across Europe
Plucked lemons for snotty faces
Plunged the stallions of madness
Through immemorial groves,
Who locked up, did not die,
Came back along the lemon track.
I would straighten, Club Foot,
I would breast you, little Carter.

viii.
I descend to vermouth and dominos.
To-night the rain thrashes indoors
Chronic viewers who forget to drink.
The fig trees are desolate.
Supper is late.
Catalan, ten years in Brazil
(Where the nuts come from)
Tells of Irish friend Wilson,
Higgins, Campbell, who hated the English.
Do I?
'The past is the past.'
Deny self. Liberal lies are bonny.
Heart whispers,
'What a whopper, honey.'
Past is not past.
More than the blessed air
It pumps into us wakefulness
Sustains ache for lilac
Long since swept down the drains.

ix.
Mother Church carries her burnt babies
Reclaimed drunk suckles delerium
Happy daddy pats his joyful solitaires
Nobel prizeman serves in trance *disjecta membra*
The fruiting fig trees croon their Master's Curse.
How could it be otherwise?

x.
Sprung from credulous loins
I'm partial to miracles.
It is not beyond the cards
(The smell of dung invades)
Fifty may find me cock
Stock and barrel successful,
Wife, kiddies, house, coins,
Many visible garlands about me.
But I say my future is failure.

Late in the night of
April Eight
Nineteen Hundred
Sixty Three
I saw it.
(Master of the Short Line, forgive me.)

xi.
Harden, Leland, John and Con,
Dickie, Paddy dear, Dara and the Swan,
Were among those who assisted at the Wake.
Take it pet from me, that was it
No resurrection or *natividad*.
O love it was truly all very sad.
(O Nati you should have been there!)
No rebudding of spent branches
No messages of hope for the peoples
Only jaded *collage* of my pat tricks
(Pardon treey bridge, swallowy garage)
And perhaps for Carroll's Special some stories:
Death at the Bridge of the Ball
By Juan Christi.

xii.
Lights out. "Franco, Franco!"
On Mont-Seny thunder fee-fa-fums,
Mongrels, pied, black, do their David.
Rain fifes, thrums and drums:
Good Lord the peace of failure.
Calm brow, cool throat, bathed limbs,
Season for the lamb, a complex beast
When you've known paper lions:
My bestiary is for sale, my love,
There are for you slashing reductions.
But may I suggest that crook-necked nag:
Give him a carrot, some hay,
Sugar at Christmas and major feasts.
If you have to bury him
Let it be far from the furious Swan.
If you have to skin him,
You may find a boy of ten
A-jingle with medals step-dancing
Tears to his mother's eyes.

(She was a school-teacher before her marriage—
This was her youngest). But
Perhaps an old nag's heart
Can take no engraving.

xiii.
Toni has come with a stranger.
Cointreau has the texture of dew.
Toni's eyes are smudged purple.
I pay the bill and through the moted air
We descend to the City of the Virgin.

Breda, Cataluña 1963—Dublin 1970

Author's notes: 'Joaquín' A young man from Galicia.
'María Antonia' Sra Puig-Bo de Piera.
'Free Cubas': Cuba libre. Spanish for rum-and-coke.
'Prici' A Barcelona eating-house.
'Nati' A Barcelona landlady.
'Toni and Mati' Sr y Sra Toni Turull.
'Harden' Mrs Harden Rodgers Jay.
'Leland' Mrs Leland Bardwell.
'John' Mr. John Jay.
'Con' Dr A.J. Levanthal.
'Dickie' Dr Richard Riordan.
'Paddy dear' Mr. P.J. Clancy. Title of a poem by Mr. James Liddy.
'Dara' Mr. Macdara Woods.
'Carroll's Special' Dr Anthony Carroll.

Excoriations on Mont-Seny . . .

Cocks crow all day on Mont-Seny:
What fowlish pleasure, what inexpressive pain?

White, blue, butterflies,
Pastel leaves,
Light on low water
Lassoing rock.

Broken cartwheels I have seen in Ireland.
But blackberries here are small and bitter.

Guardia Civil rinses mouth with soda water.
Unlike mate leaves rifle at the wall.

Rusted white church
Looks over cock
Butterfly blackberry
Water cartwheel
Guardia Civil rock
Me
O why the rifle?

Breda 1963

Facility

for Paul Durcan

O Carla little girl
in red or checkered apron
you crossed the gravel paths

You did not bring innocence
tokens only of morning
which affright the rest of the day

By now young woman
you have crossed the quarry
and hold yourself at bay

Little Carla
you are remembered
in this poem

Dublin   January 22nd 1973

A Minor Complication

High above the city of the Three Cities
The memories coalesce. Mustapha
Fiddler with electricity, stealer of bottles,
Donor of cabbages. Post-midnight knocks.
Rocks hurled by children the Prophet
Suffered to come unto Him. Hassan,
Camel meat, but was he truly *marocain?*
Suliman, bearer of wine and olives,
Incarnation of Islamic mischance,
His friend Bakush whose memories
Regrettably embrace the *palais de danse,*
Not least the Neighbour with his metherdrine,
That other ruffian and his Jacqueline.

Never again the trek to Armando's
Never again at six in the morning
The call to prayer for arid Christian buffs
Never again this afternoon of tolerable peace
When the world is governed by doves.
No vulture can take this from me.

Detail the objects on the desk.
Twenty years ago I saw that Venus,
("There she is", said Liam Ó Briain)
Seventeen years ago that Copenhagen nude,
("Get her, dear," said someone rude)
Ash-trays, the clutter of work,
An orange, Desmond's "Artemis", lean
Script that may survive the Vandals.
A match-box from Malta, *A Lonely Voice,*
All the mystery of Islam. I am too old to alter.

We do not eat *Chateaubriand*
We discuss the man.
Pushing forty in North Africa
One drops names like Goethe,
Goes on to discuss the gloomy Dane
How Rousseau might have poured into him
The desire to confess:

"Those who mess with God are not officers nor
    gentlemen".
Which brings me to a pose.
Being a minor complication a friend's life is trying,
God's minor complications happen when we are dying.

But screw the doggerel.
In the middle of the journey
I see no dark wood
Only unchanging laurels
Torrents of doves
Hurtling against the wind.

Philoctetes will be my guide
I will wear my pus like alabaster.

Tripoli, Libya 1969

Abbey Press Lunch   3/9/69

for Phil O'Kelly

Airy from early communion with Austin's monks,
Liberty Hall around the corner, I twiddle
Glass of lemony non-sin, dare not fiddle
Proscript of Antrim doctor, forbidden
Alcohol. I talk to Eamon.
Keen on priorities, he dared a Minister,
Daemon-struck, was suspended, let back in.
Long ago for a Larkin under Toto
We mummed together at Olympia.
Now we burble about ancients and Sophocles
In the Kingdom: Mac, great auk in wild earth.
I talk to Alan: not to-day nor yesterday
We had pillow-talk with Hilton:
'Two angels at my bedside!'
Low at High Table, far from Everest's brother,
I am astonished to re-call I
Lugged Laffan across *The Shadowy Waters:* he
Tells of Patrick-Tarry, Scotched in the stalls
Approached by Earnán: 'Do you remember me?'
'Indeed I do'. Blith on a hustings
Corner-boys cornered him. 'Three boos
For Blythe who never blessed himself'.
I looked down the table: Senior Critics
Serenade Hunt. But where is Gaby?
Has Fallon fallen by the wayside?
And Ó Faracháin. Has he foreseen
Fíon that without doubt is not *Gan Mhoirt?*
(At least my sip). I am happy.
Why do critics bore me, academics awe me
Editors chill me, alone poets and mummers
Throw up a Maginot Front (and we all know what came of
     that)
Against our common humanity, Huns, Vandals, all
Bent on spoliating the rose,
Redesigning the heart, converting
Tender feelings to colly-wobbles.
And of course even among the poets and mummers
There are Eichmanns and Quislings and types
Who'd be quite happy to be Ministers of Hate,

Or speculate with non-conservationists,
Or curse our beloved clergy,
Or even take a turn at harassing Hilary Boyle.
—But meandering mind damned
By something said by Vincent D.
I navigate the table and feel fond
Of Finegan, Seamus, Gus and Rushe,
Hunt's starry fays who cluster round their allocated prey
And do their job while I play with mummers.
In conclusion, Phil, while thanking you for lunch,
I've a strong hunch some of the mummers I name-drop
Will come to my funeral. Indeed
You're welcome yourself if you get a comp.
After this mild romp, outside again
To my wonderful city, and the Liffey
Seems to smell of grease-paint,
And clouds are balls of cleansing tissue
And the buses are a toccatta of Galuppi
And lamp-posts reach to the dressing-room
Of stars that, piteously, will survive my poor frail mummers.

Contra Naturam

i
I am hopeless about
Trees, shrubs, flowers:
Though I suppose
I'd parley with a dandelion or daisy
If my nose were trained
To flair nature:
A rose at a pinch.

In the main
I detest God's very own country
Wild, seed-packeted or parterred.
In my secret walks
I gibber like a loon
Against the Maker:
The wizard of waterfalls
The custodian of cataracts
The majordomo of mountains
The inventor of oaks
The generalissimo of the garden-pea.
And that goes too for
Luna clustered round with all
Her starry what d'ya callums,
Bee-loud glades, airy glens,
The Seven Bens, Everest, Etna:
All "tourist attractions"
Designed to distract from the main issue:
Our insensate captivity
Our banishment from Eden.

ii
Confession, self-analysis,
Vanity of vanities.
The air this morning
Was veined with ice.
The sky this morning
Had taken the blue-bag.
The light this morning
Was braying like a Sitwell.
I sloshed through a goulasch,
Wet brown leafage.

A brat of a dog
Leaped at me.
The beast was friendly.
A brace of copper beeches
Easy to recognise, and he
Might win me round.

Dublin 1970

Second Thoughts

Ascending descending
in the ethereal verbena
swallows dip wings
to jazzed-up *paseo*
light, light guerdon
kisses o kisses peach
the stone ochre stone
of the Church of San Pedro.
In the Holy City of Avila.

Coruscating syncopating
ebonite blackness
factitious stars emerald
ruby grenadine
mantillas in apple
waterfalls in silver
pluming smoke palm-trees
odour of cordite.
In the Holy City of Avila.

O what a squall
sent the Sierra
chair hooked table
glass ticked off bottle
little ones ululated
old ones castigated
flight of the innocents
denser the plumage of
'The Eagle of Gredos'
In the Holy City of Avila.

And I curse the turgid
Rene Füllop-Miller
easier not to know
plundered New World gold
paid the last builders' bills
for the Convent of San José.
Did Teresa ever give a damn
for the discalced Indian?
In the Holy City of Avila.

Avila   July 1971

Who Walks through Salamanca

for Pearse Hutchinson

Who walks through Salamanca
in air of bronze weightless,
forgotten, no, absolved,
the long chains of anguish
slush of three o'clock
in the etiolated mornings
merited pangs
inflicted by the meritless
exploded gladioli
diamonds cutting the panes of the heart.

Who walks through Salamanca
by platinum dreams bespangled,
apprehended, no, encompassed,
the staccati of turpitude
chill of three o'clock
in the horn-torn mornings
gratuitous goring
bulldazed by the goggled
strumpeted lilies
excremental squatting of the soul.

Who dreams in Salamanca
of the flowering body
and the fecund mind
and forgets the rest of Juvenal
the faggotry the screeching
the insatiable women,
phoenixed in bland acceptance
of 'the tragic sense of life'.
Send us Unamuño both
children of Janus
your aureoled peppery benedictions.

Salamanca   August 1971

On First Hearing of the Death of W. H. Auden

Peach, tangerine,
The clouds, the mortals,
And the bus
Toward Ròdos.

All the glitter of cats
Ignorant of passing
Departing shrouds.

The mewling icons are playing *veroñicas*
The prepuced minarets are weeping
And the conserved hinds and does
And all manner of things
Shed ironic mourning.

So do the copper-haired Graces,
The single *Suzuki* decked with carnations,
The nits in the public places
And my sprig of caraway from the mosque.

Layabout strangers
Limestone specialists
Lingering serenaders
Lament an exodus.

Myrtles are not in fashion.
I am tormented by ignorance of the names of flowers.
I pick up my match-box.
I read, 'Wistaria'.
'Wistaria', Wystan, wanhope, Wien.

Limestone into limestone.

Ròdos, 2-3 October 1973

A Note to My Auntie

The children knew even the eggs' colours,
could recognize a kind of mushroom,
might even at a pinch recognize,
nay, dear Auntie, consider the quality in trees.

You know I had a gap in my youth,
Great Masters took the mickey out of me.
Those who rot in cities
ought, should they not, have lived
in arboured, floral, turdy culture,
our country cousins in the plashy
fields of crozierdom.

Dear Auntie, was this Original Sin?

Dublin 1973

Forewarned

i.
Do you think we should measure
quality of life by prestige of stimuli?
"The power of cheap music,
'Noël, Noël?' "
Ought we anatomize if salt
Is spilt over Parma violet memories,
The seed tremor with bifurcated yen?

"Better give thanks for all feeling,
Tear in the eye for Mother Machree
Loin-shudder for lost napes
Surrogate plastic when there's no filigree."

ii.
Sex they tell us is not lust
Angelic matrons tell the lost
One-night passion turns to dust:
Sex is not a handled thigh,
Holy fathers fence the gash.
I look you in the candid eye:
Sweet Jesus, if the love-lech takes me.

iii.
And it did: and heart now croaks
And ravens and round my thigh
There's a scelus of ragwort.
My pillow is often wet
My tongue licks the postules
Of squandered kisses: stains of passion
Unseen to strangers blur my pupils.
All we can hope for now is
The Removal of the Remains.

Dublin 1969

Postscript to Patrician Stations

for Richard Riordan

No more
Like a rat in a corner.
No more
Like a bat in a trap
But luminous, humble, triumphant
I accept defeat. I know body and soul
At the feet of trencher-men, trust to the last
In honour, the solemn word, the judicious nod,
O what a sell if body and soul have gone to Pilates.
No matter   I am still
No more
Like a rat in a corner.

Dublin 1969